BOO!

OVER 150 SPOOKY JOKES!

Illustrated by Martin Chattert

MACMILLAN CHILDREN'S BOOKS

What is a baby ghost's favourite game?

Peeka-boo.

What's the difference between a deer running away and a small witch?

One's a hunted stag, the other's a stunted hag.

What is a vampire's favourite ice cream flavour?

Veinilla.

Why do witches fly on broomsticks?

Vacuum cleaner cords aren't long enough.

What fairy tale do ghosts like best?

Sleeping Boo-ty.

Why didn't the skeleton cross the road?

He didn't have the guts.

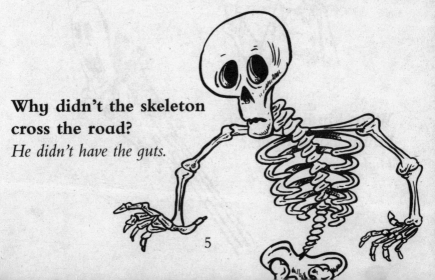

What type of dog do vampires like the best?
Bloodhounds.

Do zombies eat popcorn with their fingers?
No, they eat the fingers separately.

What kinds of ghosts haunt skyscrapers?
High spirits.

What's a monster's favourite bean?
A human bean.

What happened when the little witch was naughty at school?
She was ex-spelled.

What's red, sweet and bites people?
A jampire.

Why do mummies have trouble keeping friends?
They're too wrapped up in themselves.

How do ghosts like their eggs cooked?
Terrifried!

What do you call a dead chicken that likes to scare people?
A poultrygeist.

Mummy, Mummy, all the kids call me a werewolf!
Never mind, dear, now go and comb your face.

What goes, "Cackle, cackle, boom!"?
A witch in a minefield.

Why wasn't the vampire working?
He was on a coffin break.

What do skeletons say before eating?
Bone Appetit!

What did one ghost say to the other ghost?
"Do you believe in people?"

What kind of streets do zombies like best?
Dead ends.

Why did the vampire go to the orthodontist?
To improve his bite.

How do witches keep their hair in place while flying?
With scare spray.

What did the papa ghost say to his family when driving?
"Fasten your sheet belts."

Why don't skeletons ever go out on the town?
Because they don't have any body to go out with.

What is evil, ugly and goes round and round?
A witch in a revolving door.

**What happens
when a ghost gets
lost in the fog?**
He is mist.

**How did the glamorous
ghoul earn her living?**
She was a cover ghoul!

**What do you get when
you cross a vampire
and a snowman?**
Frostbite.

**What do they teach
at witch school?**
Spelling.

**What did Dracula
say when his
vampire girlfriend
kissed him?**
"Ouch."

**What did the
skeleton say to
the bartender?**
*"I'll have two cokes
and a mop."*

**What's big and green
and goes, "Oink, oink"?**
Frankenswine.

**What's a vampire's
favourite dance?**
The fangdango.

**What do ghosts
have for dessert?**
Ice scream.

**Why did the witch
wash her broom?**
She wanted a clean sweep.

**Who was the famous
skeleton detective?**
Sherlock Bones.

**What do you call
a lost monster?**
A where-wolf.

Where did the vampire keep his valuables?
In a blood bank.

Why don't mummies go on holidays?
They're afraid they'll relax and unwind.

What kind of spirits serve food on a plane?
Air ghostesses.

**What do witches
have races on?**
Brrrroomsticks!

**What happened to
the wolf who fell into
a washing machine?**
*He became a
wash-and-werewolf.*

**What is a skeleton's
favourite musical
instrument?**
A trombone.

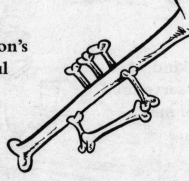

How does a girl vampire flirt?
She bats her eyes.

Why didn't the witch wear a flat cap?
There was no point in it.

**What does a
skeleton order
at a restaurant?**
Spare ribs.

**What do young
ghouls write their
homework in?**
Exorcise books!

How can you tell if a witch is carrying a timebomb?
You can hear their brooms tick.

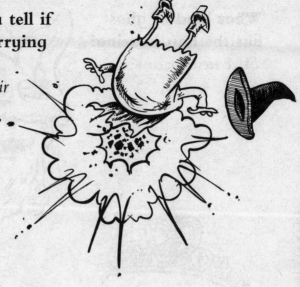

Where does Dracula have lunch?
At the casketeria.

**What kind of ghost
has the best hearing?**
The eeriest!

**Who won the skeleton
beauty contest?**
No body.

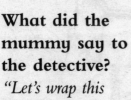

**What did the
mummy say to
the detective?**
*"Let's wrap this
case up."*

How did the witches' basketball team do?
They had a spell in the first division.

What is a mummy's favourite type of music?
Wrap!

Why doesn't anybody like Dracula?
He has a bat temper.

What ride do spirits like best at the amusement park?
The rollerghoster.

Why did the one-eyed monster have to close his school?
He only had one pupil.

How do you join the Dracula fan club?
Send your name, address and blood group.

What kind of piano music do witches play?
Hag-time.

How did the vampire marathon go?
It finished neck and neck.

**What kind of pets
do ghosts have?**
Scaredy cats.

**How do you make
a witch scratch?**
Just take away the W.

**Why do skeletons
hate winter?**
*Because the cold goes right
through them!*

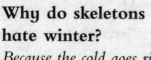

**Why shouldn't you grab
a werewolf by the tail?**
*It might be the werewolf's tail,
but it could be the end of you!*

**Why did the ghost
starch her sheet?**
*So she could scare
everyone stiff.*

**Have you heard about
the good-weather witch?**
She's forecasting sunny spells.

**Where does a ghost go
on Saturday night?**
*Anywhere where he can
boo-gie.*

**Why does Dracula
take art classes?**
He likes to draw blood.

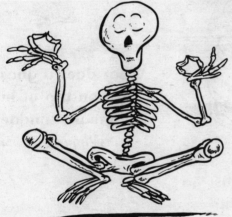

**Why are skeletons
so calm?**
*Nothing gets under
their skin.*

**What was the cold,
evil candle called?**
*The wicked wick of
the North.*

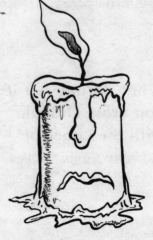

Why don't angry witches ride their brooms?
They're afraid of flying off the handle.

What does a ghost have on top of his ice cream sundae?
Whipped scream.

What do you get if you cross Dracula with Sir Lancelot?
A bite in shining armour.

**What do you call
a monster with
no neck?**
*The Lost Neck
Monster.*

**Why are so few
ghosts arrested?**
*It's impossible to pin
anything on them.*

**Why did the
skeleton jump on
a trampoline?**
*To have a rattling
good time!*

Why did the vampires cancel their cricket game?
They couldn't find their bats.

How do you get milk from a witch's cat?
Steal her saucer!

Ghost: Where do fleas go in winter?
Werewolf: Search me!

What has six legs and flies?
A witch giving her cat a lift.

What did the baby vampire bat say before going to bed?
"Turn on the dark. I'm afraid of the light!"

What do you call a stupid skeleton?
Bonehead.

What does a child monster call his parents?
Mummy and Deady.

34

What kind of ghosts haunt operating theatres?
Surgical spirits!

Why did the witch celebrate?
She passed her hex-aminations.

What is Dracula's favourite fruit?
A neck-tarine.

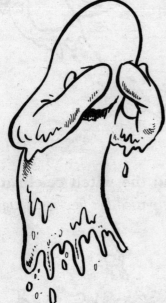

What game do ghosts play at parties?
Hide-and-shriek.

What is as sharp as a vampire's fang?
His other fang.

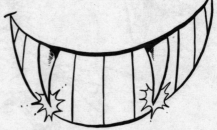

**What kind of jewellery
do witches wear?**
Charm bracelets.

**What do you
do when fifty
zombies surround
your house?**
Hope it's Halloween.

Where do ghosts post their letters?
At the ghost office.

What do you call a witch who lives at the beach?
A sand-witch.

Why are vampires like false teeth?
They come out at night.

Why do demons and ghouls hang out together?
Because demons are a ghoul's best friend!

Why did the game warden arrest the ghost?
He didn't have a haunting licence.

What do you get if you cross a witch with an iceberg?
Cold spells.

What do you get if you cross a dinosaur with a wizard?
Tyrannosaurus Hex.

Why did the skeleton stay up late studying?
He was boning up for his exams.

What do young ghosts call their mums and dads?
Transparents.

What do you call two witches who live together?
Broommates.

What is a vampire's favourite sport?
Casketball.

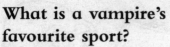

How do ghosts make a milkshake?
They sneak up behind a glass of milk and yell "Boo!"

What did the mother ghost say to her son?

"Don't spook unless you are spoken to."

Why was the witch kicked out of witching school?

Because she failed spelling.

Why are pixies such messy eaters?
Because they are always goblin their food.

How do you keep a monster from biting his nails?
Give him some screws.

Why did Dracula visit the doctor?
Because of his coffin.

What is a ghost's favourite means of transportation?
A scareplane.

Why do vampires need mouthwash?
They have bat breath.

Why did the vampire subscribe to the Wall Street Journal?
He heard it had great circulation.

What kind of make-up do ghouls wear?
Mas-scare-a.

What story do little witches like to hear at bedtime?
Ghoul deluxe and the three scares!

Why did the headless horseman go into business?
He wanted to get ahead in life.

Why do girl ghosts go on diets?
So they can keep their ghoulish figures.

**What should
you say when
you meet
a ghost?**
"How do you boo?"

**What is a ghoul's
favourite drink?**
Lemon and slime.

**Where do fashionable
ghosts shop for sheets?**
At boo-tiques.

Where does Dracula stay when he's in New York?
The Vampire State Building.

Why were ancient Egyptian children confused?
Because their daddies were mummies!

How can you tell a vampire likes baseball?
Every night he turns into a bat.

**Who was the most
famous French
skeleton?**
Napoleon Bone-apart.

**What kind of music
do ghosts prefer?**
Spirituals.

**What is a vampire's
favourite means
of transportation?**
A blood vessel.

**What do you get
if you cross a
ghost with
an owl?**
*Something that
scares people
and doesn't
give a hoot.*

**What do you call a wizard
from outer space?**
A flying sorcerer.

What does a ghoul get when he comes home late for dinner?
The cold shoulder.

Why isn't Dracula invited to many parties?
He's a pain in the neck.

Why are ghosts like newspapers?
Because they appear in sheets.

How do monsters tell their future?
They read their horrorscope.

What did the plumber say when he was called to the vampire's house?
"It's a grave problem."

**What is a ghost's
favourite party
game?**
Musical graves.

**Who did the
ghost invite
to his party?**
*Anyone he
could dig up.*

**What do wizards stop
for on motorways?**
Witchhikers.

What keeps ghouls happy?

The knowledge that every shroud has a silver lining!

Who does Dracula get letters from?

His fang club.

What happened when the ghosts went on strike?

A skeleton staff took over.

What does Dracula drink at breakfast?
Coffin with scream and sugar.

What did the ghost teacher say to her class?
"Watch the board and I'll go through it again!"

What would you get if you crossed a vampire with a snail?
I don't know, but it would slow him down.

Why did the twin witches wear name tags?
So they could tell which witch was which!

What is a ghost's favourite holiday?
April Ghoul's day.

**What airline do
ghouls fly with?**
British Scareways!

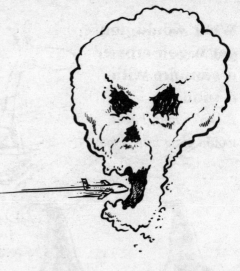

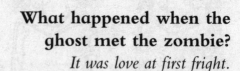

**What happened when the
ghost met the zombie?**
It was love at first fright.

**What do little
ghosts wear when
it rains?**
Boo-ts and ghoul-oshes!

What do you call a prehistoric ghost?
A terror-dactyl!

What is Dracula's favourite kind of coffee?
Decoffinated.

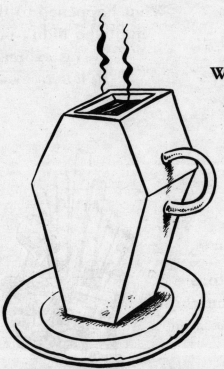

**What kind of jewels
do ghouls wear?**
Tombstones!

**What happened to the
guy who didn't pay
his exorcist?**
He was repossessed.

**Why can't skeletons
play music in church?**
Because they have no organs.

What do you give a vampire with a cold?
Coffin drops.

Where do ghosts go on holidays?
Mali-boo.

What goes "Ha, ha, ha – thud"?
A monster laughing his head off.

**What do you
call a dead cow
that's come
back to life?**
Zombeef.

**Where do
ghosts go
swimming?**
The Dead Sea.

**What does a vampire
never order at a
restaurant?**
A stake sandwich.

What do demons have for breakfast?
Devilled eggs.

What trees do ghouls like best?
Ceme-trees!

THE SIDESPLITTERS SERIES